fast and fabulous
fresh food
cookbook

Consultant Editor:
Valerie Ferguson

HERMES
HOUSE

Contents

Introduction

There is nothing to compare with fresh ingredients – lightly cooked or raw – for the quickest, tastiest and most nutritious meals. This cookbook is a joy for those of us who prefer not to spend hours in the kitchen but still desire good, flavoursome and freshly prepared food. There are light lunches or suppers and substantial meals, and you can even create a three-course dinner with the minimum of preparation. This is fast food at its most delectable and appealing.

With the wide variety of fresh ingredients available all year, the choices for quick and tasty meals are endless. Need a glamorous starter for a dinner party? Whip up Iced Tomato & Vodka Soup in record time. Looking for a special swift seafood dish? Try Swordfish with Pepper-orange Relish. Want a really quick and tasty meat or vegetarian main course? How about Lemon Chicken Stir-fry, Pear & Pecan Nut Salad with Blue Cheese Dressing or Coriander Omelette Parcels with Oriental Vegetables? And for dessert, what could be nicer than sparklingly fresh Exotic Fruit Kebabs with Mango Purée or Baked Spiced Plums with Ricotta?

Real fast and fresh food is at your fingertips in a kitchen very near you, so what are you waiting for?

Ingredients

Always buy the freshest foods you can as they will be the most nutritious – do not be tempted by 'bargains' that may be past their best.

Fresh Vegetables Stir-fried or steamed vegetables and salads are the perfect fast foods. Lightly cooked vegetables retain their crisp texture, flavour and, most important, all the nutrients. Buy locally grown vegetables where possible and use soon after purchase as storage diminishes their nutritional value.

All fresh vegetables have high amounts of vitamins, and a selection of these will provide a healthy meal. A stir-fry, for example, containing broccoli, carrots and peppers would provide vitamins A, B and E. The wider the selection of vegetables eaten, the healthier the diet will be. Choose also asparagus, avocados, beans, beansprouts, Brussels sprouts, cabbage, kale, potatoes, spinach, sweetcorn, tomatoes and watercress, for quick, healthy and tasty eating.

Fresh Fruit As with vegetables, fresh fruit is an ideal fast food. It usually does not require cooking but its versatility means that it can also be transformed into a variety of tasty dishes – both sweet and savoury. Citrus fruits, strawberries, kiwi fruit, cranberries and blackcurrants are particularly high in vitamin C, and vitamin A is also found in apricots, mangoes, peaches and melon. The wide selection of fruit now available in supermarkets means that we can choose from exotic fruits such as papayas, star fruit and pineapples as well as familiar ones.

Above: Vegetables are at their most nutritious and flavoursome when really fresh.

Herbs Fresh herbs are invaluable when you need to give an extra lift to a dish in seconds. The green leaves of chervil, chives, coriander, dill, oregano, mint, parsley, tarragon and thyme can all be used raw or lightly cooked. The cloves of garlic bulbs, which add flavour to both uncooked and cooked dishes, are reputed to have all kinds of health benefits, including warding off colds.

Pasta Fresh or dried pasta, available in a multitude of shapes and sizes, is excellent as the basis of a wholesome, satisfying meal in minutes.

Nuts & Seeds Incorporated into dishes or scattered over them as a topping, nuts and seeds are an excellent source of protein and beneficial Omega 3 and 6 oils, which can be lacking in a vegetarian diet.

Above: White and oily fish are healthy as well as quick to cook.

Fish Fresh fish needs only a short cooking time and makes wonderful fast food. All fish is rich in protein, B vitamins and minerals. Choose from white fish, such as cod, haddock, sole and plaice, or oily fish, such as sardines, mackerel, herring, tuna, trout and salmon.

Poultry, Game & Meat Choose poultry and lean, tender cuts such as pork fillet that require the minimum cooking time.

Dairy Mild cheeses such as mozzarella, ricotta and fromage frais can be used to make tasty sauces for pasta or to add to salads to make a more substantial meal.

Techniques

Blanching & Refreshing

Vegetables are blanched for several reasons: to loosen skins before peeling, to set colour and flavour, and to reduce bitterness. They are often blanched as an initial cooking when further cooking is to be done by stir-frying or a brief reheating in butter, or if they are to be used in a salad. After blanching, most foods are 'refreshed' to stop them cooking any further.

1 To blanch: immerse the food in a large pan of boiling water. Bring the water back to the boil and boil for the time specified, usually 1–2 minutes. Immediately lift the food out of the water or strain.

2 To refresh: quickly immerse the food in iced water or hold under cold running water. If the recipe specifies, leave until it has cooled completely. Drain well.

Cutting Vegetable Matchsticks

These decorative shapes, also called 'julienne', are simple to cut yet look very special.

1 Peel the vegetable and shave off curved edges. Cut across into pieces about 5 cm/2 in long. Lay each piece flat and cut it lengthways into slices 3 mm/⅛ in thick or less, guiding the side of the knife with your fingers.

2 Stack the vegetable slices and cut them lengthways into strips about 3 mm/⅛ in thick or less.

General Rules for Stir-frying

Stir-frying takes very little cooking time so it is essential that all the ingredients are prepared ahead and cut to the same size.

1 Preheat the wok for a few minutes. f using oil, allow it to heat up before dding the ingredients.

Reduce the heat a little, add the rst ingredients, then quickly increase e heat. This will keep vegetables isp and retain their colour.

Use a long-handled scoop or atula to keep the ingredients turning you stir-fry them, so that they will ok evenly and quickly.

Chopping Herbs

Many recipes require herbs to be finely or coarsely chopped; this can be done quickly following the method below. Chop herbs just before you use them as the flavour will then be at its best.

1 Remove the stalks and place the leaves on a clean, dry board. Use a large, sharp cook's knife (if you use a blunt knife you will bruise the herbs rather than slice them) and chop them until as coarse or as fine as needed.

2 Alternatively, use a herb chopper, also called a *mezzaluna,* which is a very useful tool for finely chopping herbs or vegetables and consists of a sharp, curved blade with two handles. Use the *mezzaluna* in a see-saw motion for best results.

Iced Tomato & Vodka Soup

This fresh-flavoured soup packs a punch like a frozen Bloody Mary.

Serves 4

INGREDIENTS

450 g/1 lb ripe, well-flavoured tomatoes,
 halved or roughly chopped
600 ml/1 pint/2½ cups jellied beef stock
 or consommé
1 small red onion, halved or
 roughly chopped
2 celery sticks, cut into large pieces
1 garlic clove
15 ml/1 tbsp tomato purée
10 ml/2 tsp lemon juice
10 ml/2 tsp Worcestershire sauce
handful of small basil leaves
30 ml/2 tbsp vodka
salt and freshly ground black pepper
ice cubes, 4 small celery sticks and
 sun-dried tomato bread,
 to serve

1 Put the tomatoes, stock or consommé, onion, celery, garlic and tomato purée in a blender or food processor and process to a smooth purée.

2 Press the mixture through a sieve into a bowl and stir in the lemon juice, Worcestershire sauce, basil and vodka.

3 Add salt and pepper to taste. Cover and chill. Pour the soup into individual bowls and add a few ice cubes and a celery stick to each one. Serve with sun-dried tomato bread.

COOK'S TIP: Provide more celery sticks for dipping and a jug of iced water on the table for guests to help themselves.

Gazpacho

An intense and refreshing blend of fresh vegetables and garlic.

Serves 6

INGREDIENTS

)00 g/2 lb ripe tomatoes, peeled and quartered
 cucumber, peeled and roughly chopped
2 red peppers, seeded and roughly chopped
2 garlic cloves, crushed
 75 g/6 oz/3 cups fresh white breadcrumbs
 0 ml/2 tbsp white wine vinegar
0 ml/2 tbsp sun-dried tomato purée
0 ml/6 tbsp olive oil
alt and freshly ground black pepper

O FINISH
 slice white bread
0 ml/2 tbsp olive oil
-12 ice cubes
 nall bowl of mixed chopped garnishes
    such as tomato, cucumber, red onion,
    hard-boiled egg and flat leaf parsley

1 Mix the tomatoes and cucumber in a bowl with the peppers, garlic, breadcrumbs, vinegar, tomato purée and olive oil. Season lightly with salt and pepper.

2 Process half the mixture in a blender or food processor until fairly smooth. Process the remaining mixture and mix with the first batch. Check the seasoning and add a little cold water if the soup is too thick. Chill.

3 To finish, remove the crust from the bread, and cut into cubes. Fry the bread cubes in the oil until golden. Spoon the soup into bowls, adding 1–2 ice cubes to each. Serve accompanied by the croûtons and garnishes.

Hungarian Sour Cherry Soup

Particularly popular in summer, this unusual fruit soup is served chilled.

Serves 4

INGREDIENTS
225 g/8 oz/1½ cups fresh sour or morello
    cherries, stoned
900 ml/1½ pints/3¾ cups water
50 g/2 oz/¼ cup sugar
15 ml/1 tbsp plain flour
120 ml/4 fl oz/½ cup soured cream
generous pinch of salt
5 ml/1 tsp caster sugar

1 Put the fresh, stoned cherries, water
and sugar in a pan. Poach gently for
about 10 minutes. In a bowl, blend the
flour with the soured cream; add the
salt and caster sugar.

2 Remove the cherries from the heat
and set aside 30 ml/2 tbsp of the
cooking liquid as a garnish. Stir another
30 ml/2 tbsp of the cherry liquid into
the flour and soured cream mixture,
then pour this on to the cherries.

3 Return to the heat. Bring to the
boil and simmer for 5–6 minutes.
Remove from the heat, cover and
leave to cool. Add extra salt if
necessary. Serve with the reserved
cooking liquid swirled in.

COOK'S TIP: Use only fresh
cherries as canned, frozen or bottled
ones will not taste as good.

Mango, Prawn & Tomato Vinaigrette

A light and delicious salad served with a fresh, herby dressing.

Serves 4

INGREDIENTS
1 large mango
225 g/8 oz extra-large cooked tiger prawns,
    peeled and deveined
16 cherry tomatoes, halved
fresh mint sprigs, to garnish

FOR THE DRESSING
15 ml/1 tbsp white wine vinegar
2.5 ml/½ tsp clear honey
15 ml/1 tbsp mango or apricot chutney
15 ml/1 tbsp chopped fresh mint
15 ml/1 tbsp chopped fresh lemon balm
45 ml/3 tbsp olive oil
salt and freshly ground black pepper

1 Using a sharp knife, slice off the two sides of mango, close to the stone. Remove the peel and dice all the flesh. Mix with the tiger prawns and cherry tomatoes in a bowl. Toss lightly to mix, then cover and chill.

2 To make the salad dressing, mix the wine vinegar, honey, chutney and fresh herbs in another bowl. Gradually whisk in the oil, then add salt and pepper to taste.

3 Spoon the prawn mixture into the dressing and toss lightly, then divide among serving dishes. Garnish with the fresh mint sprigs and serve.

Grilled Pepper and Goat's Cheese Salad

Colourful peppers and melting goat's cheese served on crisp salad leaves.

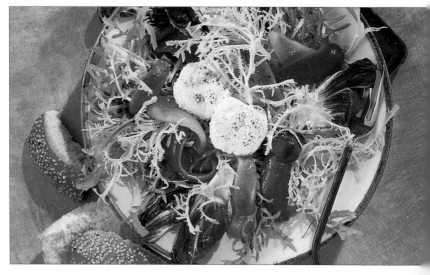

Serves 4

INGREDIENTS
1 red pepper
1 green pepper
1 yellow or orange pepper
½ radicchio, separated into leaves
½ frisée, separated into leaves
7.5 ml/1½ tsp white wine vinegar
30 ml/2 tbsp extra virgin olive oil
175 g/6 oz/¾ cup goat's cheese
salt and freshly ground black pepper

1 Preheat the grill. Cut all the peppers into pieces, discarding the seeds. Grill for 10 minutes.

2 Meanwhile, divide the radicchio and frisée leaves among four plates. Chill until required. Mix the vinegar and olive oil in a jar, season to taste and shake well.

3 Slice the goat's cheese, place on a baking sheet and grill for 1 minute. Arrange with the peppers on the salads. Pour over the dressing and grind a little extra black pepper over each.

COOK'S TIP: Serve this delicious salad for two people for a light and refreshing lunch, accompanied by fresh bread.

Spinach, Apricot & Hazelnut Salad

A nutritious and tasty salad of contrasting flavours and textures.

Serves 4

INGREDIENTS

75 g/3 oz/scant ½ cup ready-to-eat
    dried apricots
75 g/3 oz/2 cups fresh young spinach
30 ml/2 tbsp chopped hazelnuts
15 ml/1 tbsp sesame seeds
30 ml/2 tbsp orange juice
15 ml/1 tbsp balsamic vinegar
30 ml/2 tbsp plain yogurt
salt and freshly ground black pepper
crusty bread, to serve

1 Chop the apricots and place in a large bowl with the spinach and hazelnuts. Toss to mix.

2 In a small pan, heat the sesame seeds gently until they begin to colour and pop. Remove from the heat to prevent further cooking, transfer to a bowl and allow to cool.

3 Divide the salad among four plates. Mix the orange juice, vinegar and yogurt in a small bowl and season with salt and pepper. Stir in the sesame seeds. Spoon the dressing over the salad and serve with crusty bread.

VARIATION: If you prefer, sunflower seeds can be used instead of chopped hazelnuts.

15

Escabeche

This version of the classic Spanish dish combines lightly cooked fish with fresh vegetables in a piquant sauce.

Serves 6

INGREDIENTS
675–900 g/1½–2 lb white fish fillets,
    such as sole or plaice
45–60 ml/3–4 tbsp seasoned flour
vegetable oil, for shallow frying

FOR THE SAUCE
30 ml/2 tbsp vegetable oil
2.5 cm/1 in piece fresh root ginger, peeled
    and thinly sliced
2–3 garlic cloves, crushed
1 onion, cut into thin rings
½ large green pepper, seeded and cut into
    small neat squares
½ large red pepper, seeded and cut into
    small neat squares
1 carrot, cut into matchsticks
25 ml/1½ tbsp cornflour
450 ml/¾ pint/scant 2 cups water
45–60 ml/3–4 tbsp herb or
    cider vinegar
15 ml/1 tbsp light soft brown sugar
5–10 ml/1–2 tsp fish sauce
salt and freshly ground black pepper
1 small fresh chilli, seeded and sliced,
    and spring onions, finely shredded,
    to garnish (optional)
boiled rice, to serve

1 Wipe the fish fillets and leave them whole, or cut into serving portions, if you like. Pat dry on kitchen paper, then dust lightly with seasoned flour.

2 Heat the oil in a frying pan and fry the fish in batches until golden and almost cooked. Transfer to an ovenproof dish and keep warm.

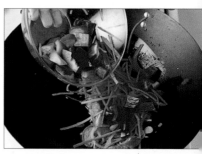

3 To make the sauce, heat the oil in a wok or large frying pan and fry the ginger, garlic and onion for about 5 minutes until the onion is transparent but not browned. Add the pepper squares and carrot strips and stir-fry for 1 minute.

4 Put the cornflour in a small bowl and add a little of the water to make a thin paste. Stir in the remaining water, the vinegar and sugar. Pour the cornflour mixture over the vegetables in the wok and stir until the sauce boils and thickens a little. Add the fish sauce and season, if needed.

COOK'S TIP: Fish sauce or *Nam Pla* is available from Asian stores and larger supermarkets.

Add the fish to the sauce and
heat briefly without stirring. Transfer
a warmed serving platter and
nish with chilli and spring onions,
ked. Serve with boiled rice.

VARIATION: Red snapper or small
sea bass could be used for this
recipe, in which case ask your
fishmonger to cut them into fillets.

Salmon Steaks with Oregano Salsa

Bursting with the fresh flavours of sun-ripened tomato and fragrant oregano, this salsa brings out the best in oven-baked salmon.

Serves 4

INGREDIENTS
15 g/½ oz/1 tbsp butter
4 salmon steaks, 225 g/8 oz each
120 ml/4 fl oz/½ cup white wine
2.5 ml/½ tsp freshly ground black pepper
225 g/8 oz ripe tomatoes
10 ml/2 tsp fresh oregano leaves, plus whole
    sprigs to garnish
4 spring onions, trimmed
30 ml/2 tbsp extra virgin olive oil
2.5 ml/½ tsp caster sugar
15 ml/1 tbsp tomato purée

1 Preheat the oven to 140°C/275°F/ Gas 1. Butter an ovenproof dish. Place the salmon steaks in the dish and add the wine and black pepper.

2 Cover the dish tightly with foil and bake in the oven for 15 minutes until the fish is just cooked. Remove from the oven and leave to cool.

3 Cut a cross in the skin at the base of each tomato. Place the tomatoes in a bowl of boiling water for 30 seconds Drain and refresh under cold water. Peel off the skin and roughly chop the tomatoes.

4 Put the oregano in a food processo and chop it very finely. Add the sprin onions, tomatoes, olive oil, sugar and tomato purée. Process in bursts until chopped but not a smooth purée.

5 Place the cold salmon on individu serving plates and pour a little of the salsa around it. Garnish each plate wi sprigs of oregano and serve.

VARIATIONS: Use white fish steaks instead of the salmon and serve them hot with the cool salsa.

Swordfish with Pepper-orange Relish

Jewel-hued sweet peppers and fresh orange juice make a wonderful relish to accompany steamed swordfish.

Serves 4

INGREDIENTS
75 ml/5 tbsp olive oil
1 large fennel bulb, cut into 5 mm/¼ in dice
1 red pepper, seeded and cut into
    5 mm/¼ in dice
1 yellow pepper, seeded and cut into
    5 mm/¼ in dice
1 orange or green pepper, seeded and cut
    into 5 mm/¼ in dice
1 small onion, cut into 5 mm/¼ in dice
5 ml/1 tsp grated orange rind
50 ml/2 fl oz/¼ cup fresh orange juice
4 pieces swordfish steak, about
    150 g/5 oz each
salt
fresh chives, to garnish

2 Stir in the orange rind and juice and cook for 1 minute more. Stir in 2.5 ml/½ tsp salt. Cover and set aside.

3 Bring some water to the boil in the bottom of a steamer. Meanwhile, brush the fish steaks on both sides with the remaining oil and season with salt.

1 Heat 45 ml/3 tbsp of the oil in a large, non-stick frying pan. Add the fennel, peppers and onion and cook over medium heat for about 5 minutes until just tender and still crunchy.

COOK'S TIP: Swordfish is a full-flavoured fish which benefits from simple cooking, as here. Frozen swordfish, however, does not have such a good flavour.

4 Place the fish steaks in the top part of the steamer. Cover the pan and steam for about 5 minutes until the steaks are opaque throughout.

5 Transfer the fish to individual serving plates. Serve immediately, accompanied by the pepper-orange relish and garnished with chives.

Stir-fried Prawns with Mangetouts

A very simple-to-cook and pretty dish, which is delicious served on a bed of rice noodles. The ingredients are cooked for the minimum time to retain all their flavour and texture.

Serves 4

INGREDIENTS
300 ml/½ pint/1¼ cups fish stock
350 g/12 oz raw tiger prawns,
    peeled and deveined
15 ml/1 tbsp vegetable oil
1 garlic clove,
    finely chopped
225 g/8 oz/2 cups mangetouts
1.5 ml/¼ tsp salt
15 ml/1 tbsp dry sherry
15 ml/1 tbsp oyster sauce
5 ml/1 tsp cornflour
5 ml/1 tsp caster sugar
15 ml/1 tbsp cold water
1.5 ml/¼ tsp sesame oil

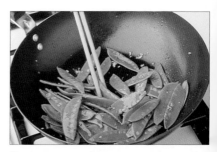

2 Heat the vegetable oil in the non-stick frying pan or wok. Add the chopped garlic and cook for a few seconds, then add the mangetouts. Sprinkle with the salt. Stir-fry for 1 minute.

1 Bring the fish stock to the boil in a frying pan or wok. Add the prawns. Cook gently for 2 minutes until the prawns have turned pink, then drain and set aside.

3 Add the prawns and sherry to the pan or wok. Stir-fry for a few seconds, then add the oyster sauce. Mix the cornflour and sugar to a paste with the water. Add to the pan and cook, stirring constantly, until the sauce thickens. Drizzle with the sesame oil and serve.

Seafood Conchiglie

This warm salad is composed of scallops, pasta and fresh rocket and flavoured with roasted pepper, chilli and balsamic vinegar.

Serves 4

INGREDIENTS
8 large fresh scallops
300 g/11 oz/2¾ cups dried conchiglie
15 ml/1 tbsp olive oil
15 g/½ oz/1 tbsp butter
120 ml/4 fl oz/½ cup dry white wine
90 g/3½ oz rocket leaves,
    stalks trimmed
salt and freshly ground black pepper

FOR THE VINAIGRETTE
60 ml/4 tbsp extra virgin olive oil
15 ml/1 tbsp balsamic vinegar
1 piece bottled roasted pepper, drained and
    finely chopped
1–2 fresh red chillies, seeded and chopped
1 garlic clove, crushed
5–10 ml/1–2 tsp clear honey, to taste

1 Cut each scallop into two or three pieces. If the corals are attached, pull them off and cut each piece in half. Season the scallops and corals with salt and pepper.

2 To make the vinaigrette, put the oil, vinegar, chopped pepper and chillies in a jug with the garlic and honey and whisk well.

3 Cook the conchiglie in a large saucepan of boiling salted water according to the instructions on the packet, until *al dente*.

4 Meanwhile, heat the oil and butter in a non-stick frying pan until sizzling. Add half the scallops and toss over a high heat for 2 minutes. Remove with a slotted spoon and keep warm. Cook the remaining scallops in the same way.

COOK'S TIP: Use only fresh scallops for this dish – they are available all year round in most fishmongers and from fish counters in supermarkets. Frozen scallops tend to be watery and tasteless, and frequently prove to be rubbery when cooked.

Add the wine to the liquid
remaining in the pan and stir over a
high heat until the mixture has
reduced to a few tablespoons. Remove
from the heat and keep warm.

6 Drain the pasta and tip it into a
warmed bowl. Add the rocket, scallops,
the reduced cooking juices and the
vinaigrette and toss well to combine.
Serve immediately.

25

Tuna, Chick-pea & Cherry Tomato Salad

A quick and easy salad that makes a satisfying light meal when served with thick slices of wholemeal bread.

Serves 6

INGREDIENTS
5 ml/1 tsp olive oil
1 garlic clove, crushed
5 ml/1 tsp ground coriander
5 ml/1 tsp garam masala
5 ml/1 tsp hot chilli powder
120 ml/4 fl oz/½ cup
 tomato juice
30 ml/2 tbsp balsamic vinegar
dash of Tabasco sauce
675 g/1½ lb cherry tomatoes, halved
½ cucumber, sliced
1 bunch radishes, sliced
1 bunch spring onions, chopped
50 g/2 oz watercress, trimmed
2 x 400 g/14 oz cans chick-peas,
 drained and rinsed
15 ml/1 tbsp chopped
 fresh parsley
15 ml/1 tbsp chopped
 fresh chives
400 g/14 oz can tuna in brine, drained
 and flaked
salt and freshly ground
 black pepper

1 Heat the olive oil in a small saucepan. Add the crushed garlic and spices and cook gently for 1 minute, stirring continuously.

2 Stir in the tomato juice, vinegar and Tabasco sauce and heat gently until the mixture is boiling. Remove the pan from the heat and set aside to cool slightly.

3 Put the tomatoes and cucumber in a serving bowl. Add the radishes, spring onions and watercress. Stir in the chick-peas and herbs.

VARIATION: Replace the chick-peas with canned red kidney or cannellini beans, if you prefer.

4 Pour the tomato dressing over the salad and toss the ingredients together to mix. Add the tuna, season to taste with salt and freshly ground black pepper and serve immediately.

Pasta Salade Niçoise

In this salad the ingredients of a classic French salade Niçoise are given a modern Italian twist with the use of penne pasta and fresh instead of canned tuna.

Serves 4

INGREDIENTS

115 g/4 oz French beans, topped,
    tailed and cut into 5 cm/2 in lengths
250 g/9 oz/2¼ cups dried
    penne rigate
105 ml/7 tbsp extra virgin olive oil
2 fresh tuna steaks, total weight
    350–450 g/12 oz–1 lb
6 baby Italian plum tomatoes,
    quartered lengthways
50 g/2 oz/½ cup pitted black olives,
    halved lengthways
6 bottled or canned anchovies in olive oil,
    drained and chopped
30–45 ml/2–3 tbsp chopped fresh
    flat leaf parsley, to taste
juice of ½–1 lemon, to taste
2 heads of chicory, leaves separated
salt and freshly ground
    black pepper
lemon wedges, to serve

1 Cook the French beans in a large pan of boiling salted water for 5–6 minutes. Remove the beans using a large slotted spoon and refresh under cold running water.

2 Add the pasta to the pan of bean cooking water, bring back to the boil and cook according to the instructions on the packet until *al dente*.

3 Meanwhile, heat a ridged cast-iron pan over a low heat. Dip a wad of kitchen paper in the oil, wipe it over the surface of the pan and heat gently. Brush the tuna steaks on both sides with oil and sprinkle liberally with pepper; add to the pan and cook over a medium to high heat for 1–2 minutes on each side. Remove and set aside.

4 Drain the cooked pasta well and ti into a large bowl. Add the remaining oil, the beans, tomato quarters, black olives, anchovies, parsley, lemon juice, and salt and pepper to taste. Toss well to mix, then leave to cool.

5 Flake or slice the tuna into large pieces, discarding the skin, then fold into the salad. Taste the salad and adju the seasoning as necessary. Arrange th chicory leaves around the inside of a large, shallow bowl. Spoon the pasta salad into the centre and serve with lemon wedges.

Lemon Chicken Stir-fry

In this speedily prepared dish, fresh lemon really brings out the flavour of the chicken, which might otherwise seem rather bland.

Serves 4

INGREDIENTS
4 boned and skinned chicken breasts
15 ml/1 tbsp light soy sauce
75 ml/5 tbsp cornflour
1 lemon
60 ml/4 tbsp olive oil
1 bunch spring onions, cut diagonally
    into 1 cm/½ in lengths
1 garlic clove, crushed
15 ml/1 tbsp caster sugar
about 30 ml/2 tbsp dry sherry
about 150 ml/¼ pint/⅔ cup chicken stock
salt and freshly ground black pepper
salad leaves and lemon wedges, to serve

1 Divide each chicken breast into two natural fillets. Place between two sheets of clear film and flatten to a thickness of 5 mm/¼ in with a rolling pin.

2 Cut into 2.5 cm/1 in strips. Put the chicken into a shallow dish with the soy sauce and toss. Sprinkle over 60 ml/ 4 tbsp cornflour to coat each piece.

3 Using a swivel peeler, remove the lemon rind in thin strips and cut into fine shreds. Squeeze the lemon juice. Blend the remaining cornflour to a thin paste with water.

4 Heat the oil in a wok or large frying pan and cook the chicken very quickly in small batches for 3–4 minutes until lightly coloured. Remove and keep warm while frying the rest of the chicken.

5 Add the spring onions and garlic t the pan and cook for 2 minutes. Add the sugar, sherry, stock and cornflour paste, stirring until thickened.

Add the lemon shreds, then return the chicken to the pan. Add more sherry or stock if necessary and stir until the chicken is evenly covered with sauce. Reheat for 2 more minutes. Serve immediately, accompanied by salad leaves and lemon wedges.

VARIATIONS: This dish would also be delicious using pork tenderloin or fillet. The flavour of the pork goes particularly well with orange in place of the lemon.

For a substantial meal, accompany the dish with egg noodles tossed in a little sesame oil and soy sauce.

Chicken with Asparagus

Asparagus is an ideal partner for chicken as their flavours complement each other so well.

Serves 4

INGREDIENTS
4 large boned and skinned
   chicken breasts
15 ml/1 tbsp ground coriander
30 ml/2 tbsp olive oil
20 slender asparagus spears, cut into
   7.5–10 cm/3–4 in lengths
300 ml/½ pint/1¼ cups
   chicken stock
15 ml/1 tbsp cornflour
15 ml/1 tbsp lemon juice
salt and freshly ground
   black pepper
15 ml/1 tbsp chopped fresh parsley,
   to garnish

2 Heat the oil in a large frying pan and fry the chicken very quickly in small batches for 3–4 minutes until lightly coloured. Season each batch with a little salt and freshly ground black pepper. Remove and keep warm while frying the rest of the chicken.

1 Divide the chicken breasts into two natural fillets. Place each between two sheets of clear film and flatten to a thickness of 5 mm/¼ in with a rolling pin. Cut into 2.5 cm/1 in strips diagonally across the fillets. Sprinkle over the ground coriander and toss to coat each piece.

3 Add the asparagus and chicken stock to the pan and bring to the boil. Cook for a further 4–5 minutes or until tender.

COOK'S TIP: To prepare asparagus, cut off the woody ends, then scrape the white part with a knife.

4 Mix the cornflour to a thin paste with a little cold water and stir into the sauce to thicken. Return the cooked chicken to the pan together with the lemon juice. Reheat and then serve immediately, garnished with chopped parsley.

Orange Chicken Salad

Tangy orange segments, toasted cashew nuts and rice combine with tender chicken in this tasty salad, which is best served at room temperature.

Serves 4

INGREDIENTS

3 large seedless oranges
175 g/6 oz/scant 1 cup long grain rice
475 ml/16 fl oz/2 cups water
10 ml/2 tsp Dijon mustard
2.5 ml/½ tsp caster sugar
175 ml/6 fl oz/¾ cup vinaigrette dressing
   (see Cook's Tip)
450 g/1 lb cooked chicken, diced
45 ml/3 tbsp snipped fresh chives
75 g/3 oz/¾ cup cashew nuts, toasted
salt and freshly ground black pepper
mixed salad leaves, to serve

2 Put the pieces of orange rind in a saucepan and add the rice. Pour in the water, add a pinch of salt and bring to the boil. Cover and cook over a very low heat for 15–18 minutes or until the rice is tender and all the water has been absorbed.

1 Pare one orange thinly, taking care to remove only the coloured part of the rind and avoiding the bitter pith.

COOK'S TIP: To make vinaigrette dressing, whisk 45 ml/3 tbsp red wine vinegar with salt and pepper to taste. Gradually whisk in 90 ml/6 tbsp corn oil and 60 ml/4 tbsp olive oil.

3 Meanwhile, cut the peel from all the oranges. Working over a plate to catch the juices, cut each segment away from the surrounding membrane. Add the orange juice, mustard and sugar to the vinaigrette dressing and whisk to combine well. Taste and add more salt and pepper if needed.

When the rice is cooked, remove it om the heat and discard the orange nd. Spoon the rice into a bowl, let it ol slightly, then add half the dressing. oss well and leave to cool completely.

5 Add the chicken, chives, cashew nuts and orange segments to the rice in the bowl. Add the remaining dressing and toss gently. Serve on a bed of mixed salad leaves.

Duck Breasts with Red Plums, Cinnamon & Coriander

Sealing the duck breasts briefly over a high heat before cooking them in the oven locks in all the delicious juices.

Serves 4

INGREDIENTS

4 duck breasts, about 175 g/6 oz
  each, skinned
10 ml/2 tsp crushed cinnamon stick
50 g/2 oz/4 tbsp butter
15 ml/1 tbsp plum brandy
  or Cognac
250 ml/8 fl oz/1 cup chicken stock
250 ml/8 fl oz/1 cup double cream
6 fresh red plums, stoned and sliced
6 fresh coriander sprigs, plus extra
  to garnish
salt and freshly ground
  black pepper

2 Melt half the butter in a large frying pan and fry the skinned duck breasts quickly on both sides to seal. Transfer to a shallow ovenproof dish with the butter and bake for 10–15 minutes.

3 Remove the dish from the oven and return the contents to the pan. Add the plum brandy or Cognac and set it alight. When the flames have died down, remove the duck from the pan and keep warm.

4 Add the stock and cream to the pan and simmer gently until reduced and thick. Season to taste.

1 Preheat the oven to 190°C/375°F/ Gas 5. Score the duck breasts, sprinkle with salt and press the crushed cinnamon on to both sides.

5 In a pan, melt the remaining butter and fry the sliced plums and coriander sprigs just long enough to cook the fruit through.

Arrrange the duck breasts on erving plates and pour some sauce round each one. Garnish with the lum slices and a few coriander sprigs, nd serve.

VARIATION: Fresh apricots would also work well in place of the plums. Skin them, if you like, by soaking them in boiling water for 30 seconds.

Sweet-&-sour Pork Stir-fry

This is a great idea for a quick family supper. Remember to cut the carrots into thin strips so that they cook in time.

Serves 4

INGREDIENTS
450 g/1 lb pork fillet
30 ml/2 tbsp plain flour
45 ml/3 tbsp oil
1 onion, roughly chopped
1 garlic clove, crushed
1 green pepper, seeded and sliced
350 g/12 oz carrots, cut
    into strips
225 g/8 oz can bamboo
    shoots, drained
15 ml/1 tbsp white wine vinegar
15 ml/1 tbsp soft brown sugar
10 ml/2 tsp tomato purée
30 ml/2 tbsp light soy sauce
salt and freshly ground
    black pepper

2 Heat the oil in a wok or large frying pan and cook the pork over a medium heat for about 5 minutes until golden and cooked through. Remove with a slotted spoon and drain on kitchen paper. You may need to do this in batches.

3 Add the onion and garlic to the pan and cook for 3 minutes. Stir in the green pepper and carrots and stir-fry over a high heat for 6–8 minutes or until the vegetables are beginning to soften slightly.

1 Thinly slice the pork. Place the flour in a bowl and season well. Add the pork and toss to coat.

4 Return the meat to the pan with the bamboo shoots. Mix the remaining ingredients with 120 ml/4 fl oz/½ cup water, add to the pan and bring to the boil.

5 Simmer gently for 2–3 minutes or until piping hot. Adjust the seasoning, if necessary, and serve immediately.

Spring Vegetable Stir-fry

A colourful, dazzling medley of fresh and sweet young vegetables.

Serves 4

INGREDIENTS
15 ml/1 tbsp peanut oil
1 garlic clove, sliced
2.5 cm/1 in piece fresh root ginger, peeled
    and finely chopped
115 g/4 oz baby carrots
115 g/4 oz patty pan squash
115 g/4 oz baby sweetcorn
115 g/4 oz French beans, topped and tailed
115 g/4 oz sugar snap peas, topped and tailed
115 g/4 oz young asparagus, cut into
    7.5 cm/3 in pieces
8 spring onions, trimmed and cut into
    5 cm/2 in pieces
115 g/4 oz cherry tomatoes

FOR THE DRESSING
juice of 2 limes
15 ml/1 tbsp runny honey
15 ml/1 tbsp soy sauce
5 ml/1 tsp sesame oil

1 Heat the oil in a wok or frying pan. Add the garlic and ginger and stir-fry over a high heat for 1 minute.

2 Add the carrots, patty pan squash, sweetcorn and beans and stir-fry for another 3–4 minutes.

3 Add the sugar snap peas, asparagus, spring onions and cherry tomatoes and stir-fry for a further 1–2 minutes.

4 To make the dressing, put the lime juice, honey, soy sauce and sesame oil in a small bowl and mix thoroughly. Add to the pan.

VARIATION: You could use any fresh, crunchy vegetables for this stir-fry. Try broccoli florets, courgettes or mangetouts.

5 Stir well, then cover the pan. Cook for 2–3 minutes more until the vegetables are just tender but still crisp. Serve immediately.

Vegetables Julienne with a Red Pepper Coulis

Just the right dish for vegetable lovers. Choose a selection of your favourite vegetables, cut them into equal-size finger lengths and steam them over aromatic, bubbling water.

Serves 2

INGREDIENTS
selection of vegetables (choose from
    carrots, turnips, asparagus, parsnips,
    courgettes, green beans, broccoli, salsify,
    cauliflower, mangetouts)
sprigs of fresh thyme
2 bay leaves
fresh green herbs, to garnish

FOR THE RED PEPPER COULIS
1 small onion, chopped
1 garlic clove, crushed
15 ml/1 tbsp sunflower oil
15 ml/1 tbsp water
3 red peppers, roasted, skinned, seeded
    and chopped
120 ml/8 tbsp fromage frais
squeeze of fresh lemon juice
salt and freshly ground
    black pepper

1 Prepare all the vegetables and cut them into thin fingers or small, bite-size pieces.

2 To make the coulis, lightly sauté the onion and crushed garlic in the oil and water for 3 minutes. Add the chopped red peppers and cook for a further 2 minutes.

3 Process the coulis in a food processor or blender, then work in the fromage frais, lemon juice and seasoning to taste.

4 In a saucepan, bring some water to the boil with the thyme and bay leaves. Fit a steamer over the top.

5 Arrange the prepared vegetables on the steamer. Place the harder root vegetables at the bottom and steam these for about 3 minutes.

VARIATION: The red pepper coulis makes a wonderful sauce for many other dishes. Try it spooned over fresh pasta with lightly steamed or fried courgettes, as a jacket potato topping, or use it as a pouring sauce for savoury filled crêpes.

6 Add the other vegetables to the steamer according to their natural tenderness and cook for a further 2–4 minutes.

7 Divide the vegetables among individual serving plates with the sauce to one side. Garnish with fresh green herbs, and serve.

Coriander Omelette Parcels with Oriental Vegetables

Stir-fried vegetables in black bean sauce make a remarkably good omelette filling, which is quick and easy to prepare.

Serves 4

INGREDIENTS
130 g/4½ oz broccoli, cut into
   small florets
30 ml/2 tbsp groundnut oil
1 cm/½ in piece fresh root ginger, peeled and
   finely grated
1 large garlic clove, crushed
2 fresh red chillies, seeded and
   finely sliced
4 spring onions, sliced diagonally
175 g/6 oz/3 cups pak choi, shredded
50 g/2 oz/3 cups fresh coriander leaves,
   plus extra to garnish
115 g/4 oz/½ cup beansprouts
45 ml/3 tbsp black bean sauce
4 eggs
salt and freshly ground
   black pepper

1 Blanch the broccoli in boiling salted water for 2 minutes. Drain, then refresh under cold running water.

2 Meanwhile, heat 15 ml/1 tbsp of the oil in a frying pan or wok. Add the ginger, garlic and half the chillies and stir-fry for 1 minute. Add the spring onions, broccoli and pak choi and stir-fry for 2 minutes more, tossing the vegetables continuously to prevent sticking and to cook them evenly.

3 Chop three-quarters of the coriander and add to the frying pan or wok. Add the beansprouts and stir-fry for 1 minute, then add the black bean sauce and heat through for 1 minute more. Remove the pan from the heat and keep warm.

4 In a bowl, mix the eggs lightly with a fork and season well. Heat a little of the remaining oil in a small frying pan and add a quarter of the beaten egg. Swirl the egg until it covers the base of the pan, then scatter over a quarter of the remaining coriander leaves. Cook until set.

5 Turn out the omelette on to a plate and keep warm while you make three more omelettes in the same way, adding more oil when necessary.

6 Spoon the vegetable stir-fry on to the coriander omelettes and roll up. Cut in half crossways and serve garnished with coriander leaves and the remaining chilli.

Pasta with Green Vegetable Sauce

Although described as *sugo* in Italian, this is not a true sauce because it does have any liquid apart from the oil and melted butter. It is more a medley of vegetables. Tossed with freshly cooked pasta, it is ideal for a fresh and light lunch or supper.

Serves 4

INGREDIENTS
2 carrots
1 courgette
75 g/3 oz French beans
1 small leek
2 ripe Italian plum tomatoes
1 handful fresh flat leaf parsley
25 g/1 oz/2 tbsp butter
45 ml/3 tbsp extra virgin olive oil
2.5 ml/½ tsp granulated sugar
115 g/4 oz/1 cup frozen peas
450 g/1 lb/4 cups dried pasta,
    such as rigatoni
salt and freshly ground black pepper
deep fried parsley, to garnish

1 Dice the carrots and the courgette finely. Top and tail the French beans, then cut them in half. Slice the leek thinly. Peel and dice the tomatoes. Chop the fresh flat leaf parsley and set aside.

2 Heat the butter and oil in a frying pan. When the mixture sizzles, add the prepared leek and carrots. Sprinkle the sugar over and fry, stirring frequently, for about 5 minutes.

3 Stir in the courgette, French beans, peas and plenty of salt and pepper. Cover the pan and cook over a low to medium heat for 5–8 minutes until the vegetables are tender, stirring occasionally.

4 Stir in the tomatoes and chopped parsley. Taste the mixture and adjust the seasoning as necessary.

Cook the pasta in a large pan of boiling salted water according to the instructions on the packet until *al dente*. Drain, toss with the vegetables and serve garnished with parsley.

VARIATION: This dish could also be made using diced red, green and yellow peppers with the courgette, French beans, tomatoes and leek.

Penne with Rocket & Mozzarella

Use the freshest ingredients possible for this simple but flavoursome dish.

Serves 4

INGREDIENTS
400 g/14 oz/3½ cups fresh or
    dried penne
6 ripe Italian plum tomatoes, peeled,
    seeded and diced
2 x 150 g/5 oz packets mozzarella cheese,
    drained and diced
2 large handfuls rocket,
    total weight about 150 g/5 oz
75 ml/5 tbsp extra virgin olive oil
salt and freshly ground
    black pepper

1 Cook the pasta in a large saucepan of boiling salted water according to instructions on the packet until *al dente.*

2 Meanwhile, put the tomatoes, mozzarella, rocket and olive oil into a large bowl with a little salt and pepper to taste and toss well to mix.

3 Drain the cooked pasta and tip it into the bowl. Toss well to mix and serve immediately.

Right: Penne with Rocket & Mozzarella (top); Eliche with Chargrilled Peppers

Eliche with Chargrilled Peppers

A high summer dish when peppers and tomatoes are plentiful.

Serves 4

INGREDIENTS
3 large peppers (red, yellow and orange)
350 g/12 oz/3 cups fresh or dried eliche
    or fusilli
1–2 garlic cloves, to taste, finely chopped
60 ml/4 tbsp extra virgin olive oil
4 ripe Italian plum tomatoes, peeled, seeded
    and diced
50 g/2 oz/½ cup pitted black olives, halved
    or quartered lengthways
1 handful fresh basil leaves
salt and freshly ground
    black pepper

1 Grill the peppers under a hot grill for about 10 minutes, turning frequently until charred. Place in a plastic bag, seal and leave to cool. Peel off the charred skins, split the peppers open and discard the seeds.

2 Cook the pasta in a large saucepan of boiling salted water according to the instructions on the packet until *al dente.* Thinly slice the peppers and place them in a large bowl with the remaining ingredients and seasoning. Drain the pasta and add to the bowl. Toss to mix and serve immediately.

Conchiglie from Pisa

Nothing could be more simple than hot pasta tossed with fresh, ripe tomatoes, ricotta and sweet basil.

Serves 4–6

INGREDIENTS
350 g/12 oz/3 cups dried conchiglie
130 g/4½ oz/generous ½ cup ricotta cheese
6 ripe Italian plum tomatoes, diced
2 garlic cloves, crushed
1 handful fresh basil leaves, shredded, plus
   extra whole leaves to garnish
60 ml/4 tbsp extra virgin olive oil
salt and freshly ground black pepper

1 Cook the pasta in a large saucepan of boiling salted water according to the instructions on the packet until *al dente.*

2 Meanwhile, put the ricotta cheese into a large bowl and mash with a fork until smooth.

3 Add the tomatoes, garlic and basil, with salt and pepper, and mix well. Add the olive oil and whisk thoroughly. Taste and adjust the seasoning as necessary.

4 Drain the cooked pasta, tip it into the ricotta mixture and toss well to mix. Garnish with basil leaves and serve immediately.

VARIATION: An avocado is the ideal ingredient for adding extra colour and flavour to this pasta dish Halve, stone and peel, then dice the flesh. Toss it with the hot pasta at the last minute.

Sesame Noodle Salad

Toasted sesame oil adds a nutty flavour to this Oriental-style salad.

Serves 2–4

INGREDIENTS

200 g/7 oz/1 cup sugar snap peas
250 g/9 oz medium egg noodles
2 carrots, cut into julienne strips
2 tomatoes, seeded and diced
30 ml/2 tbsp chopped fresh coriander, plus
    extra whole leaves to garnish
15 ml/1 tbsp sesame seeds
3 spring onions, shredded
salt

FOR THE DRESSING
10 ml/2 tsp light soy sauce
30 ml/2 tbsp toasted sesame seed oil
15 ml/1 tbsp sunflower oil
cm/1½ in piece fresh root ginger, peeled
    and finely grated
garlic clove, crushed

1 Slice the sugar snap peas diagonally. Place the noodles in a saucepan of boiling lightly salted water and bring back to the boil. Cook for 2 minutes, then add the sugar snap peas and cook for a further 2 minutes. Drain and rinse under cold running water.

2 Meanwhile, combine the dressing ingredients in a screw-top jar or bowl. Shake or mix to combine thoroughly.

3 Tip the noodles and the peas into a large bowl and add the carrots, tomatoes and chopped coriander. Pour over the dressing and toss with your hands to combine. Serve warm, sprinkled with the sesame seeds and spring onions, and garnished with whole coriander leaves.

Spring Vegetable Salad

This chunky salad makes a satisfying meal, using waxy, new potatoes. Other spring vegetables can be added, if you like.

Serves 4

INGREDIENTS
675 g/1½ lb small new potatoes, halved
225 g/8 oz/2 cups young broad beans
   (shelled weight)
115 g/4 oz cherry tomatoes
50 g/2 oz/½ cup walnut halves
30 ml/2 tbsp white wine vinegar
15 ml/1 tbsp wholegrain mustard
60 ml/4 tbsp olive oil
pinch of sugar
225 g/8 oz young asparagus
   spears, trimmed
6 spring onions, trimmed
salt and freshly ground
   black pepper
baby spinach leaves,
   to serve

1 Put the potatoes in a pan. Cover with cold water and bring to the boil. Cook for 10–12 minutes until they are almost tender.

2 In another pan, cook the broad beans in boiling salted water for about 3 minutes. Drain, cool under cold running water and drain again.

COOK'S TIP: If time permits, you can slit the skins of the broad beans and pop out the green beans.

3 Tip the broad beans into a large bowl. Cut the cherry tomatoes in half and add them to the bowl with the walnuts.

4 Put the vinegar, mustard, oil and sugar into a screw-top jar. Add salt and pepper to taste. Close the jar tightly and shake well.

5 Add the asparagus to the potatoes and cook for 3 minutes more. Drain the cooked vegetables well, cool under cold running water and drain again. Thickly slice the potatoes. Cut the spring onions into halves lengthways

6 Add the asparagus, potatoes and spring onions to the bowl containing the broad bean mixture. Pour the dressing over the salad and toss well to combine the ingredients thoroughly. Serve the salad on a bed of baby spinach leaves.

Fattoush

This Middle Eastern mixed salad is traditionally topped with pieces of unleavened bread to soak up the dressing. It provides the perfect solution of what to do with slightly stale pitta breads.

Serves 4

INGREDIENTS
2 wholemeal pitta breads
1 iceberg or cos lettuce, torn
 into pieces
1 green pepper, seeded
10 cm/4 in piece cucumber
4 tomatoes
4 spring onions
a few black olives, to garnish

FOR THE DRESSING
60 ml/4 tbsp olive oil
45 ml/3 tbsp lemon juice
2 garlic cloves, crushed
45 ml/3 tbsp finely chopped fresh parsley
30 ml/2 tbsp finely chopped fresh mint
few drops of harissa or chilli
 sauce (optional)
salt and freshly ground black pepper

1 Grill or toast the pitta breads on both sides until crisp and golden. Cut into rough squares and set aside.

2 Place the lettuce in a large bowl. Chop the green pepper, cucumber, tomatoes and spring onions roughly, making sure that they are all about the same size. Add them to the lettuce and toss together well.

3 To make the dressing, put the olive oil, lemon juice, garlic, parsley and mint into a screw-top jar. Add the harissa or chilli sauce, if using, and seasoning. Close the jar tightly and shake well.

4 Just before serving the dish, pour the dressing from the jar over the salad and toss well to mix together. Scatter pieces of pitta bread over the salad, garnish with the black olives and serve.

VARIATION: Any salad leaves can be used instead of lettuce. Try young spinach leaves, rocket or Swiss chard, for a change.

Pear & Pecan Nut Salad with Blue Cheese Dressing

Toasted pecan nuts have a special affinity with crisp white pears.

Serves 4

INGREDIENTS
75 g/3 oz/³⁄₄ cup shelled pecan nuts
3 crisp pears
175 g/6 oz young spinach,
   stems removed
1 escarole or butterhead lettuce
1 radicchio
salt and freshly ground black pepper
crusty bread, to serve

FOR THE DRESSING
75 g/3 oz blue cheese, rind removed
150 ml/¼ pint/²⁄₃ cup plain yogurt
45 ml/3 tbsp olive oil
30 ml/2 tbsp lemon juice
15 ml/1 tbsp snipped fresh chives

1 To make the dressing, mash the blue cheese with one-third of the yogurt in a bowl. Stir in the remaining ingredients and season with pepper.

2 Toast the pecan nuts under a moderate grill to bring out their flavour. Cut the pears into even slices and discard the cores.

3 Place the salad leaves in a large bowl. Add the pears and toasted pecans. Pour over 30–45 ml/2–3 tbsp of the dressing (chill the rest for use in another recipe) and toss well. Distribute among four serving plates and season with salt and pepper. Serve with warm crusty bread.

Orange & Avocado Salad

A super salad of crisp and sharp, soft and sweet, fruity and nutty flavours.

Serves 4

INGREDIENTS
90 ml/6 tbsp olive oil
15 ml/1 tbsp walnut oil
45 ml/3 tbsp lemon juice
30 ml/2 tbsp orange juice
5 ml/1 tsp grated orange rind
5 ml/1 tsp Dijon mustard
pinch of caster sugar
salt and freshly ground black pepper
1 round lettuce
1 small bunch watercress
few leaves of frisée
1 small bunch of rocket
1 red onion, thinly sliced into rings
2 seedless oranges, peeled and segmented
1 ripe avocado, peeled, stoned and cubed
50 g/2 oz/½ cup walnut pieces, toasted

1 To make the dressing, put the first seven ingredients into a screw-top jar. Season, close the jar and shake well.

2 Put all the salad leaves into a large bowl and add the onion, orange segments and avocado. Pour over the dressing and toss the salad to combine well. Scatter the walnuts on top and serve immediately.

Exotic Fruit Salad

Passion fruit makes a superb dressing for any fruit, but really brings out the flavour of exotic varieties.

Serves 6

INGREDIENTS
1 mango
1 papaya
2 kiwi fruit
coconut or vanilla ice cream, to serve

FOR THE DRESSING
3 passion fruit
thinly pared rind and juice of 1 lime
5 ml/1 tsp hazelnut or walnut oil
15 ml/1 tbsp clear honey

1 Peel the mango, cut it into three slices, then cut the flesh into chunks. Peel the papaya and cut it in half. Scoop out the seeds, then chop the flesh. Place both fruits in a large bowl.

2 Cut both ends off each kiwi fruit, then stand them on a board. Using a small, sharp knife, cut off the skin from top to bottom. Cut each kiwi fruit in half lengthways, then cut into thick slices. Add to the bowl.

3 To make the dressing, cut each passion fruit in half and scoop the seeds out into a sieve set over a small bowl. Press the seeds well to extract all their juices. Lightly whisk the remaining dressing ingredients into the passion fruit.

4 Pour the dressing over the fruit and mix gently to combine. Chill before serving with scoops of coconut or vanilla ice cream.

Lemon-grass Skewers

Kebabs of aromatic exotic fruit are ideal for a barbecue.

Serves 4

INGREDIENTS

4 long fresh lemon grass stalks
1 mango, peeled, stoned and cut
   into chunks
1 papaya, peeled, seeded and cut
   into chunks
1 star fruit, cut into thick slices
8 fresh bay leaves
butter, for greasing
freshly grated nutmeg
60 ml/4 tbsp maple syrup
50 g/2 oz/¼ cup demerara sugar
150 g/5 oz/⅔ cup curd cheese or
   low-fat soft cheese
120 ml/4 fl oz/½ cup
   double cream
grated rind and juice of ½ lime
30 ml/2 tbsp icing sugar

1 Prepare the barbecue or preheat the grill. Cut the top of each lemon grass stalk into a point with a sharp knife. Discard the outer leaves, then use the back of the knife to bruise the length of each stalk to release the aromatic oils. Thread each stalk, skewer-style, with the fruit pieces and bay leaves.

2 Cover a baking sheet with foil, roll up the edges to make a rim. Grease the foil, lay the kebabs on top and grate some nutmeg over each. Drizzle with maple syrup and dust with demerara sugar. Barbecue or grill for 5 minutes until lightly charred.

3 Mix together the cheese, cream, lime rind and juice, and icing sugar in a bowl. Serve with the kebabs.

Pineapple Wedges with Allspice & Lime

Fresh pineapple is easy to prepare and always looks very festive so this dish is perfect for easy entertaining.

Serves 4

INGREDIENTS
1 medium ripe pineapple
1 lime
15 ml/1 tbsp dark muscovado sugar
5 ml/1 tsp ground allspice

1 Using a sharp knife, cut the pineapple lengthways into quarters and remove the core.

2 Loosen the flesh by sliding a knife between the flesh and the skin. Cut the flesh into slices, and replace it on to the skin.

3 Using a swivel peeler, remove a few thin pieces of rind from the lime and cut into fine shreds. Squeeze the juice from the lime.

4 Sprinkle the pineapple with the lime juice and rind, sugar and allspice. Serve immediately, or chill briefly.

VARIATION: For a hot dish, place the pineapple slices on a baking sheet, sprinkle them with the lime juice, sugar and allspice and place them under a hot grill for 3–4 minutes. Sprinkle with lime rind and serve.

Baked Spiced Plums with Ricotta

Star anise has a warm, rich flavour – if you cannot get it, try ground cinnamon instead. A wonderful dish for cooler late-summer evenings.

Serves 4

INGREDIENTS
butter, for greasing
450 g/1 lb ripe red plums, halved
    and stoned
115 g/4 oz/½ cup ricotta cheese or
    fromage frais
15 ml/1 tbsp caster sugar
2.5 ml/½ tsp ground star anise

1 Preheat the oven to 220°C/425°F/
Gas 7. Grease a wide, shallow
ovenproof dish.

2 Arrange the plums, cut side up, in
the dish. Using a teaspoon, spoon
some ricotta cheese or fromage frais
into the hollow of each plum. Sprinkle
with the sugar and star anise.

3 Bake the filled plums in the oven
for 15–20 minutes or until they are
hot and bubbling. Serve warm.

VARIATION: This recipe also
works well with peaches or
nectarines instead of plums.

Exotic Fruit Kebabs with Mango Purée

Fresh fruit makes the easiest, healthiest dessert you can find – you can choose whatever fruit is in season.

Serves 4

INGREDIENTS
1 ripe mango, peeled, stoned
   and chopped
15 ml/1 tbsp lime juice
½ small pineapple, cored
1 guava or papaya, peeled
   and seeded
2 kiwi fruit, peeled and quartered

1 Place the chopped mango and lime juice in a food processor and blend until smooth.

2 Cut the pineapple and guava or papaya into bite-size chunks and thread on to four bamboo skewers along with the kiwi fruit.

3 To serve, spoon a little mango purée on to four serving plates and place a kebab on top.

VARIATION: For a change, large strawberries, when in season, are particularly good as substitutes for the kiwi fruit.

Red Fruits in Filo Baskets

Light-as-air filo pastry is very easy to use. Colourful summer fruits stirred into creamy yogurt are the perfect filling.

Serves 4

INGREDIENTS
3 sheets filo pastry, thawed if frozen
10 ml/2 tsp sunflower oil
115 g/4 oz/1 cup mixed red summer fruits, such as raspberries, redcurrants, strawberries
150 g/5 oz/⅔ cup Greek-style yogurt

1 Preheat the oven to 200°C/400°F/ Gas 6. Lightly brush each sheet of filo pastry with oil, then cut them into 12 pieces, each 10 cm/4 in square.

2 Keep the unused squares of filo pastry covered with a clean, damp cloth while you make the baskets. Line four small patty tins with three overlapping squares of filo pastry. Bake for 6–8 minutes, until crisp and golden brown. Remove from the oven, leave to cool, then turn out on to a wire rack.

3 Reserve a few pieces of fruit for decoration, then stir the remaining fruit into the yogurt. Spoon the yogurt into the filo baskets and decorate with the reserved fruit. Serve immediately.

This edition is published by Hermes House

Hermes House is an imprint of Anness Publishing Ltd
Hermes House, 88–89 Blackfriars Road, London SE1 8HA
tel. 020 7401 2077; fax 020 7633 9499; info@anness.com

A CIP catalogue record for this book is available from the British Library.

Publisher: Joanna Lorenz
Editor: Valerie Ferguson
Series Designer: Bobbie Colgate Stone
Designer: Andrew Heath
Editorial Reader: Marion Wilson
Production Controller: Joanna King
Recipes contributed by: Catherine Atkinson, Carla Capalbo, Jacqueline Clark, Trish Davis,
Matthew Drennan, Sarah Edmonds, Christine France, Nicola Graimes, Deh-Ta Hsuing,
Norma MacMillan, Sue Maggs, Kathy Man, Maggie Mayhew, Norma Miller, Sallie Morris, Annie Nichc
Maggie Pannell, Katherine Richmond, Anne Sheasby, Laura Washburn, Steven Wheeler.
Photography: William Adams-Lingwood, Karl Adamson, Edward Allwright, Mickie Dowie,
James Duncan, Joanna Farrow, John Freeman, Ian Garlick, Michelle Garrett, Amanda Heywood,
Janine Hosegood, David Jordan, Don Last, Thomas Odulate.

Previously published as *Fast & Fresh Cookbook*

Notes:
For all recipes, quantities are given in both metric and imperial measures and,
where appropriate, measures are also given in standard cups and spoons.
Follow one set, but not a mixture, because they are not interchangeable.
Standard spoon and cup measures are level.
1 tsp = 5 ml   1 tbsp = 15 ml
1 cup = 250 ml/8 fl oz
Australian standard tablespoons are 20 ml.
Australian readers should use 3 tsp in place of
1 tbsp for measuring small quantities of gelatine, cornflour, salt etc.
Medium eggs are used unless otherwise stated.

1 3 5 7 9 10 8 6 4 2